MELTING
FROZEN GLOW

Rajbir Deswal

BOOKS FOR ALL

Delhi

Author: Rajbir Deswal

First Published 2013

ISBN 13: 978-81-7386-298-4
ISBN 10: 81-7386-298-2

Published By

BOOKS FOR ALL

A-6, Second Floor, Nimri Commercial Centre,
Ashok Vihar Phase-4, Delhi - 110 052 (India)
Tel.: +91 11 2730 2453 Fax: +91 11 4706 1936
website: www.Lppindia.com
e-mail: info@Lppindia.com

Printed At
D K Fine Art Press P Ltd.
Delhi-110052

Sawan Deswal's photo of Snoqualmie Pass, Seattle on the cover

PRINTED IN INDIA

To

Anaysa & Armaan

Editorial

I have just finished reading with interest Rajbir Deswal's latest collection of poems. It is his tenth book and the fourth collection of poems in English, the other being his *My Own Khajuraho* (2012), which I have had the pleasure of going through with great curiosity and engross.

Rajbir Deswal, an IPS officer of Haryana cadre, is a prolific writer and a leading columnist, who regularly keeps writing Middles for a number of national Dailies, such as *The Tribune, The Times of India, Hindustan Times, The Indian Express* and *Daily Post* and yet he finds time to bring out books on varied subjects from time to time.

Deswal's latest collection of English poems, comprises of more than 165 poems — a tall order. At the heart of his poetic craft is his great passion, animation, fervour and zest, for each composition itself speaks of his enthusiasm and his devotion to the poetic craft, and his earnestness, which all combine to make the end-product highly readable.

A close look on the entire collection reveals that the subject-matter or main themes of these poems are as varied as Deswal's own mood—sometimes exuberant, sometimes effervescent, fulsome, attentive, heedful, introspective, spiritualist, mystic, philosophic etc. etc.

Like a raconteur, he graphically draws a picture of a cold January day, when a dense cloak of fog rushes in of its own from some unnoticed crevice. On such a cold morning, no man or woman can be seen out, no child is playing hooky. Even birds like coots and herns do not move out of their small but cosy nests. The leaves on boughs, too, do not stir. In such a season, when Nature seems at rest, the poet's eye in Deswal grabs it for picturesque delineation.

In another shorter poem titled 'Work in progress', a very common sight, the opening line is 'Men at work', but in the immediately following lines the poet raises a question: "How about women/who work too?". It's a thought-provoking question. A child (possibly of those working on the road engaged in its repair or carpeting) is described sucking his thumb silently and peacefully on the naked ground by the roadside. The poet calls it a 'make-do cradle'. Indeed, this is modern poetry or rather a specimen of post modernism. His poetic craft is for anyone, who can stand and watch such men and women and children in this increasingly self-centered, complex and shrinking world.

Further, in the poem titled 'Life's Way', Deswal philosophically says: "Even when you call it a day/Soul still holds its sway". This is prima facie an expression of mysticism, so to say.

In *Melting Frozen Glow* the description of "incandescent frozen glow gradually melting down" through a dreamy insubstantial town is breathtaking. It rings "a pageant of melody", which is sublime, elevating and uplifting.

There are many such examples to quote from the present poetic collection, but for reasons of space crunch I have to leave these for the readers themselves to find out.

Nevertheless, for all the seriousness of his themes, Deswal is a keen observer of Nature, of clouds, of rain and of men and women around. He speaks plainly and with great emotional intelligence. He writes in simple, plain language, and can *ipso-facto* easily connect with his readers and critics alike.

Often his rhyming schemes get mixed up with free verse or blank verse. He knows what T.S. Eliot (1888-1965) and William Carlos Williams (1883-1963) maintained that free verse is not entirely free. As such, Deswal devises a rhythm of natural speech.

As an accomplished poet, he has become a platform with his pastiche for a new generation of poets, experimenting with many new forms, themes, rhythms and by mixing these with free verse and blank verse.

I congratulate him for his present endeavour and wish him all luck for future too.

Deepak Tandon

A Comment

I have had the pleasure and privilege of knowing Mr. Rajbir Deswal for many years now. He is a unique being who combines in him the seriousness of his calling, the humor and wit of his writing, and what is more the warmth and openness of his personality. How he does it with elan and finesse, I won't ever know. So, I know and know him not – somewhat in the manner of Derridean appropriation of sign!

Deswal towers over many as a writer of insightful articles on contemporary issues, travelogues and reviews of books, and above all, humorous 'Middles' appearing regularly in various national dailies which are enjoyed by a vast number of readers. Now, an artist is an artist and various genres provide him but different vistas for the expression of his multi-faceted talent. His taking to writing of poetry has to be appreciated in this context.

Like his 'Middles', most of the poems in *Melting Frozen Glow* are also fully pregnant with deep insight. A number of poems happen to originate in the course of Deswal's indulgence in his blog and other internet platforms, where wit is the staple of numberless ephemeral feeds. Nevertheless, it must be said to his credit that he is able to turn these feeds miracolously into sumptuous food for thought that lingers behind, not in the digestive, but cerebral tracts for a long time.

Melting Frozen Glow focusses on myriad experiences. The poet has always had the privilege to live and experience that to which others are by Nature insensitive: 'Sleep-walking mind speaks/Of wide-eyed escapades/Ogling, groping in gleam/To lull me into consciousness.' A number of poems express philosophical musings; one such is 'Full Circle Full': Life's magic full with spell/Spell full with suspense/Suspense full with fear/Fear full with anger/Anger full with disgust...' and so it goes on to join the other emotional links in the chain of mundane experiences to reach *ur*-humanity finally. This is the cycle of *maya*, as our scriptures tell us, which keeps us engrossed in worldly life.

A large chunk of poems concerns Nature. Deswal sings of seasons in the vein of romantic poets – with child-like glee and enthusiasm: 'Rain does the road enliven/ Trampled, trodden, dubbed, driven/Also lets it cool its nerves/ O how saviour like it serves/ Roughness gone, feel silken.' Rain-drops seem to have a special fascination for the poet. In one of his Middles, I remember, he reminisces about a street in his village which was inundated during the monsoon and which he waded through, merely for the sake of re-living the childhood days! It is no surprise, therefore, to read in his poem of raindrops on electricity wires which 'hold and balance them there...beginning to slide the slope/ stop awhile/ roll again/ fall finally.'

Shifting to the metaphorical plane, the poet watches wistfully, as it were, the coalescing of the droplets of moments into 'running, relaying, rolling carpets.' Ruefully, not everyone in the contemporary world has the inclination (forget the excuse of time) to stand and stare the way Deswal does. Rightly therefore, he holds out sane advice to the cut-throat competitors of the world: 'One must give up/One must yield/Not just to bat/But also to field.' Indeed, one must learn to take one's call, for come Fall (autumn) and the leaves 'leave their moorings, gladly fall'!

Deswal impresses with his rich diction. The opening poem gives an idea of his choice of words—delicate and musical—in keeping with the choice of subject: 'Incandescent frozen glow gradually melting down. Flowing through insubstantial dreamy town...' Deswal's forte is visual imagery closely followed by its auditory version. He also goes in for synesthetic imagery when he claims to touch a tinkle and hear a touch! Besides, his poetic art is hitched steadfastly to alliteration so much so that he does not mind glossing over grammatical niceties, but then which poet does not take that liberty!

In some poems, the lure of rhyme has impelled the poet to experiment with colloquialism though the underlying thought is lofty enough to turn it into a classy limerick: 'Happy mind, painful gut/ One too wanting, other glut/ Years to yearn, years to live/ Less to take, more to give/ Much before one goes phut.'

Even in this compilation of mainly light verse with pieces like 'Time to heal/ Time to steal', one comes across some outstanding poems like the one in which the passing night has been compared to a river joining the sea *a la* T.S. Eliot's 'Four Quartets' with 'bass notes of night/ and treble notes of day/ fall into an eternal warp of time and keep creating music.' That is trying to capture eternity and timelessness! We hope to have more such poems from Mr. Deswal!

Jagdish Batra

Introduction and Acknowledgements

That I have edited all the ten books written by Rajbir Deswal, makes me modest enough, to admit the fact of my having a near-handicap in not being able to treat his poetry, with the same set of gloves. I have always liked to add a serious note to the author's near-gimmickry which should be taken in the right earnest; I being an admirer and a critic not only at hand, but at home too—literally. There are certain writing projects that we jointly undertake but poetry of Rajbir Deswal has an exclusive and unique domain, diction and direction.

Dr. Deepak Tandon, a renowned litterateur in North India taught American literature, poetry and Shakespearean drama for about 20 years to students pursuing their Masters and Doctorates in English. He has a great passion for Urdu poetry and has presented papers in innumerbale seminars and symposia. For the last about 30 years he has been writing on important issues in various national dailies. Mr. Khushwant Singh has written about Dr. Tandon in laudatory terms many times in his columns. Very shortly a book is likely to hit the stands which *inter alia* will have correspondence between the two masters, stretched over about three decades. A very fine human being, Dr. Tandon is suave, gentle and personable besides being an erudite scholar. He has lent his master-strokes in *Melting Frozen Glow*. Rajbir Deswal's earlier anthology *My Own Khajuraho* also had a taste of Dr. Tandon's pen in fine tuning quite a few of the poetic creations of the author.

Dr. Jagdish Batra is an Emeritus Professor of JJT University, Rajasthan who presently heads the English Language Centre at OP Jindal Global University, Sonepat. He has authored three books and edited two anthologies of critical essays, all on English literature. A known academic of long standing, Dr. Batra has guided many Ph.D. scholars, conducted workshops and has organised many conferences. He also headed the PG department of English, Hindu college, Sonepat. Dr. Batra is also known for his social work and taking up issues in public interest. A man of many parts, he has acted in films besides having remained actively engaged in philanthropic works in association with the Rotary Club and Haryana Jaycees.

Rajbir Deswal's poetry seems to be a take on his own style of writing prose in a lyrical form. That he experiments with the unknown, unexplored finer nuances and grammar of writing poetry, needs to be discounted in favour of his passion to sing and revel in his keen observation of things worldly, mundane, mystical, spiritual and divine. Other than English, his anthologies in Hindi and Urdu have also come out in recent past and have been taken with aplomb by his admirers and critics alike. *Taron ke Jungle, Bareshein Girti Rahin* and *Rehguzar* being cases in point. Deswal's depiction of things around him, and those emanating from his deep inner observations, may not be analytical but they fit the bill and are creatively remarkable, meeting the standards set by experts and professionals.

The frozen glow is melting in your hands now to make your own impression. It sure does inspire and tickle in its own poetic way!

Chander Koumdi

My Turn

Poems I do not make
They make me a man
Make me think, feel
Observe, open my eyes
If and when they can
Ring in my ears,
Touch me, tease me
Load me with words
Which I give back
Tasted, treated, tailored
Making mild statements
Maybe only to myself,
Maybe only for myself
They mean to me a lot
And I look at them endearingly
As one does ones own child
And a poem is made, spelt
Frozen glow begins to melt

Rajbir Deswal

Contents

The way life is

Spiritual hues

Roll of seasons

Body & mind

Gypsy time

In nature's lap

Melting Frozen Glow

Incandescent frozen glow gradually melting down
Flowing through insubstantial dreamy town;
Sublime, elevating, uplifting
A pageant of melody rings
In air, with colourful springs;
Breeze oozing soft red-vine like taste
Still, serene, placid, soulful n' chaste;
Lilting, lulling as though rocking to sleep;
Stirring pulses with soft cushiony touch
To make one sing on and yet on
O, that incandescent frozen glow gradually melting down

Poet's Eye

This January morn is cold, O, very cold
Thick fog rushes in of its own
From every crevice it can find
Brining shivers for young and old
No man or woman in the street
No hooky child out
A breathless hush pervades all around
Dormant they seem but ever watchful
Leaves on boughs don't rustle
Coots and herns move not among ferns
O, Nature at its rest
But in me's awake a poet's eye

Rock On

Tiny Lilliputian droplets of rain hang about,
Hang around, and hang high
— and keep shining
Till someone had a look
And Lo! They drop
Having really rocked
Have a look!

Appearance

The sun grows under a shade
Abandoned, drained of light
Tones change of light and shade
Now dark, now bright?
Here's that perceptions fade

Green & Red

Turning red is here for sure
Reason to be enough mature
Living life with grind n' gall
Pith and green, gone with fall
Making still as good manure
Nature's law, clarion call

Another Breather

Starfish having been swept ashore
Mother Earth offers it her lap
To let it grow, flourish galore
Offering new life, one time more

Beam-Watch

It's not just illusory though it seems
Trickling, treading of rays, beams
Dark gives way to yellow flames
Me enjoying their gremlin games
Glow-patterns bursting at seams

Nature's Treasures

Bliss bounties
Unbound, purest, disarming
Impelling an attendant feel
Of blessedness
Unabated, endless,
Enduring, effusing
Lighting up
With the speed and strength of
A ray—radiant and resplendent
With light and hope
Of contentment
Quenched, filled, brimmed with
Bliss bounties

Biting Dust

Nights seen to hide
Days to lay all bare
Perceptions deride
With least care
Of what night n' day
Swear on time
Curse you and I may
Their toothy mime
Still they're true
Being what they are
You and me to rue
What you and I are
Being to both unfair
Them and us, all
We take it as ours
What's Nature's call
Explain it on our terms
Ravish it being ruthless
Explore it till the berms
Biting being toothless

Shades of Colours

Colours have their shades too
To offer if they wanting look
Colours have their combos new
To add to hueless life's book
Colours rainbow's dear ones
Lose to other—losing oneself
Watery despair's hopeful suns
A dab, a tinge, same as self

Beauty

Petals soft, fragrant or no
Pith and pulp, sponge or snow
Patterns of hues, patches too
Pokin' beckonin' lurin' to woo
Prithee! Pause, look at the glow

Lazying

Night-air being still
The leaves too chill
Asleep, taking turns
Moth and the ferns
Enjoy attendant quiet
To wake when it's bright

Rained Out

It's a morning cool, cool, O, very cool
Office, business, shop, or school
Treated with complacent ease
Not to torture not to tease
Happy rains soak the rule

Moony

From pale of glow
Slip slow n slow
To shine on sable
Light up, enable
Lunar shadow

Building Hope

All through the night
It roared and poured
Morn sees streams
Bright
Residual watery dreams
In sight
Realizing in icicles
Frozen snow-white
But in shiny nickels
Crystal moments
To make the day—after night

Healing Touch

Better burn within,
With agonizing pain
Or a pail full of hails
Treat putting one
On each blister
Cool heal, make 'm happy,
Let regale
Only a healthy scar
Will register
Ev'n less than a gale
Not a blizzard to take on
But budging a bit
To let pass
Fail

Day Break

Night whispers
Begin to be heard
By the dawn
Only to be hushed
By bird tweets
And some
Freshly coloured rays

High In Air

Whacky wind fetches a whiff, from the vale
Where it flew flawless, like swim of a whale
Sliding, sloping, singing, swinging, swaggering
Smiling, dancing, frolicking rocking; steadily
Floating, over the cloud's large cottony bale

Rain Hope

Clouds truly ignored again,
Pouring drops of beautiful rain
Nature we need to know full well
Looks sanguine where hopes dwell
Clouds sure will float again
Blessing the land with beautiful rain

Rivulet

Flows past a stream
Glows fast a dream
Gurgles, vistas and a feel
Sliding, slipping like eel
Lullabies full of gleam

Beating Heat

Before they're about to abort
Things too ticklish need we sort
Sun's raising hell through heat
A cool cucumber needed to beat

Stellar World

Stars are gluttons
They dine and shine
Till dawn, they burp twinkles
Beginning last evening, fine

Hills Call

Call of the hills—there!
I hear, 'Here, here!'
Roll up, slide down
Cheer, fresh air
Here! Here!

Sustenance

All seeds germinate
With roots to go down
Trunk n' branches to go up
One for grip
The other for growth

Morning Music

The lark I don't hear
But twinkle on water
Sleeping in a pond
Lushed by soft breeze
To stir up
Caressing its wet cheeks
Beckoning the lark
To awaken—chirrup
Lo! It speaks—garrulous!

The way life is

Wish

Glint, sparkle, beam, ray
Keep gross gloom ever at bay
Liven up, brighten bloom full
All your life just this way

Exhumed

Digging out Earth's maiden deep
Letting savour outer space, feel
It knew no beams, no light, no turn
Only colour known to it was dark
Done—undone, undone—done

Conformity

If only I could endorse
A seconding ditto
On a dotted line
For not conforming
To what I felt
Should've stayed joined
As it was, where it was

Bonds

Foreign souls' plastic smile
Our's own, a bit demure
Human bonds not to revile
Callow blood too to mature
One to one, no censure

Openings

Gloomy heart gladdens
When gaiety flattens
Junk from rigid cockles
Beating blues with batons
Candles, diyas are too much

First Step

Dipping heart does have a start
Inner-eye looking outwards
Feelings pop and hold a stake
When utterly fail the words
Sooth and smooth is all velvet
For Joggers, walkers stewards
Tugs, yarns still make carpet
Keep walking ever, forwards

High Head

Standing tall
Despite the fall
Nature's way
To gaily say
Rise to fall
Is no way small

Transition

One must give up
One must yield
Not just to bat
But also to field
With your turn
You live with hope
Hope you live with
Despair to burn
Hope and wish
Though seldom go
Hand in hand
Through and through
Grab a moment
Live it wholesome
Good to handover
Others, to welcome

Wait & Go

Waiting for the bus together
Waving, being left alone
Leave you must if and whether
Wait again to set a tone
Waving a wait, letting a gone!

Lit Up Shadow

If you have a beam of light
With me a little out in tow
You can surely see through bright
Lighting up my shadow

Mismatch

Setting foot for alien lands
Connecting with my own hands
Much to delight much to miss
Many shades of happy sands
Shingling, mingling, tingling bands

Life's Book

Turning pages, dawning days
Back and forth, many ways
Moro to see, yest to look
Read-unread life's book
Or white-fish to have its ways

Father and Son

Opening eyes, emitting light
Breathing life a bit shyly
Claims its slice and the bite
Of darkness rising merrily
Sun dawns blithesome bright
Makes a rosy promise—gaily
A Father-figure kidding; Right?
Gets born as a kid, cheerfully

Helping Hand

To tie is the very purpose of thread
To beat hunger is hard earned bread
To give and help a hand must know
To toil with sweat on the eyebrow
They never exploit who're thorough bred

Life's Motion

Pacing slow, when need be
Fine movement, good speed be
Rest and restless both need care
Stillness into the act to stare
Deep into living life, to let it be

Cliffhangers

Slowing showers turn to pour
Harvested, rested drops galore
Light-ball from every cusp slips
Glowing, gleaming rolls, drips
More of less, less of more

Happy Hard-Work

Happy mind, painful gut
One too wanting, other glut
Years to yearn, years to live
Less to take, more to give
Much before one goes phut

Grey Areas

Not really a peep, ringside view,
All that's seen looks anew
Black is white, white is black
Still nasty does it smack
'Peek-a-boo; I see you!'

Scribble

Neither smarting epic
Nor lampooning comic
Being true to topic
Not being myopic
Keep drawing wordpic

Confidence

When if you think you're gone
When if you're told you're done
Look within, stop for a while
Give yourself a fulsome smile
Tell yourself you're second to none

Danger Ahead

More pitfalls on risky roads!
Who will take care of these kids?
Is it necessary to fall in a pit?
And then invite attention
Of media and authorities
Are they not exposed to risk?

Soluble

What is to thaw is to find form
Of love, affection care and concern
What it is to melt is prettier still
That's held in form, is let spill
Again to find a form, from form

Walling In, Out

My wall is a wall, not a slate
Where you come just to berate
And then turn away, go back straight
Without paying due freight
For carrying your unwieldy weight
Making me with disgust, gyrate
To raise issues healthy for debate
No ill-will, animosity to create
Come you must here, but wait!
To make the wall livelier, O, my mate!

Binding Hold

Holding in a bind, binding in a hold
Selling of a kind and kind of hold
Getting in a grind n' getting of gold
Sealing of life as if it's sold
Saying Bard's 'Life a tale by an idiot told'
Seeing maybe watching, only to behold
Living it always as if cajoled
Dreaming ever over rose-bed rolled

Selflessly

O how nice it is to know
What good it does to others
What we at times keep doing
Unmindfully, for others

Pampering

Filled largely with frustration
Till a few droplets come
Saying—'Hey come'n smile again!'
And you find frustration gone
With happy thoughts, on and on

Dawning

Mild glow of morning time
Ticks too but tickles more
Whispering same yesternight lullabies
With featherlike sun rays
Half-heartedly playing notes
Stroking hair to let eyes stay closed
Before the day breaks
And the Sun stands astride the world
—astounding, waking up

Jelled

Drift or drive away
Separation has a way
Parts akin not to part
Moorings still to stay
In the life's effusion
Flowing, oozing in unison
A bond that binds, jelled
Still holding on to fusion
Even when you call it a day
Soul still holds its sway
Or is it the times, memories
Things?— that happened everyday!

Smiles

Something within makes you smile
Outwardly smiles smell too vile
Smiles manmade are though honest
Baby smiling looks the most best
Some smiles go mile and mile
Not to doubt but as jester's beguile

Get, Set, Go!

Part by part,
Set to depart
Heave a sigh
Have a heart
Pick up dart
Another start
Sprint 'n go
Be smart

Enduring

Goes there the saying
Old is gold, staying
Vouching for relevance of
Things that keep staying

Wing Reeds

Yeats, Keats, Whitman and Donne
Told me nothing in person, none
Same for Neeraj, Faiz, Iqbal
Sheharyaar, Amrita, Sahir et al
Majrooh, Faraz, Ghalib, Momin
Evenin with them and my monin

Solary-G

Somewhere Sun-u bright-u, bright-u
Otherwhere Sun-u dark-u
Somewhere enuf light-u light-u
Otherwhere nat a spark-u
Why this soulless-Solary-G

Full Circle

Life's magic full with mystic spell
Spell brimful with suspense
And with unknown fear
Fear full with rage
Anger full with disgust
Rage full with hatred
Hatred with self-pity
Self-pity with remorse
Remorse loaded with hope
Hope full of promise
Promise with commitment
Commitment with faithfulness
Faithfulness with devotion
Devotion with prayer
Prayer with compassion
Compassion with love
Love with godliness
Godliness with humanity
Humanity full with humbleness
That completes circle of life

Disconnect

Seeing on ground a wing
Even though shed, gone dead
Worries me a lot, thinking
About the beautiful bird
About notes it used to sing

Guts

A heavy heart
Is counselled to
Take things light
Prick or dart
Or even a bolt
From the blue
One can't but
Suffers the jolt
A heavy heart
Is a heavy heart

Me, Myself

They made 'yours truly'
Purposely poorer by an 'e'
Saving on vowels
Throwing in towels
As true as the word
Expecting me to be

Work In Progress

Men at work!
How about women?
Who work too
And the child
On that make-do cradle
With its thumb in mouth
Silently braving the chill
On a naked ground
By the roadside

At It Again

Sometimes
Even for
An ensuing
Or impending
Longish gap,
You windup
As you do
At the end
Of it all!
And
Maybe
You start
Afresh
Later
As if
Nothing occured
In between
And nothing
Began
At all

Coin's Two Sides

Watery drop has a sable side too
Moonlike, with stony looks too
Contrasts always are no paradox
Soft is the lie, how so sweetly true

Haze & Hunger

Fearing filtering in fog of the squeak
Little chics keep tweaks in the beak
Fire within will compel it soon
'Mama get something ere its noon!'
Chic-chic-chic-chic-chic-chic-cheek

Economy

Gleaming rays
Fall on deaf ears
Do not return
Echo assumes airs
Light, sound, turns
Just a show of
Diminishing returns

Drones

No sweat, no gain
No threat, no pain
Lives there the man
Drubbing his life-span
Turning sides—again

Alleviated

What is dull is heavy too
Difficult to lift in one go
Light, light throw some weight
Dullness not let heavy grow

Hunger

To make believe, sure that
Verily there's, the cat
Obliqueing the pigeon out
No temptation wish'd or sought
Nothingness set to fraught

Introspection

Looking inward once in a while, I think
Which verse is one well-versed in
Not any, to me it occurs, none !
Looking inward, there's always a blink

Luxurious

Talking to oneself
Daydreaming
Aren't just hallucinations
But only for others
To see and mull
—on a clear day
When all's quiet
And leisurely dull

Light & Sound

Capable of nourishing
I think is light divine
As divine word cures
With tune set in rhyme
Nothing visual or aural
But only inwardly divine

Girl Child Day

Speaks softly a ray
Mumbles a prattle
To her teddy
Blabbers croons
Hums tunes
Making my day

Spiritual hues

Prayers

Some songs classic-like forever last,
Are holier than an epic chant,
Or rosaries beads in willing hands,
Oozing bliss from beaded bands;
On lips a musical chant of hymn
Cleansing self through invocation to Him
Stirring harmony, lasting peace
Let songs of soul keep echo along

Suns

Beads bid bouyance sun entering them
Beads say prayers thread running in
Beads touch fingers to let feel divine
Beads on all sides throw their shine
Beads make rosary sing divine hymn

Rumi

Use could you me
If there was no Rumi
Minus his wisdom
And my humdrum
Blaring blurbs boomy

Godliness

To keep Him on His highs
We keep heaving sighs
Sometimes cold, at others hot
We give Him too, do we not?
Meek or bold everyone tries
Seeking ever, looking upto skies

Earth and Sky

Earth's the sky for the flying
They drop out here dying
Like we look upto the sky
When to earth we say good bye

Gongs

O ye jingling wind chimes
Sweet notes at all times
Care freely rendered tunes
Redeeming, cleansing grimes

One To One

I don't really know if soul
That came to irrigate the parched self
Of the one in his mortal frame
Is anxious again
To be with Him in His Domain
But here soul
Made one see the light within
To the one who wouldn't feel
Anything on his skin
But only worldly feel
Of pleasure and pain
Soul to soul seems to be the goal

Kindly Light

Out of the many good things about light
The most kindliest is its
Ability and proclivity
To reflect in balanced measures
The light that a medium
Expects from it—fine-tuning tight

O' God!

Divine is what is ordained
Divine is what is obtained
Divine is what is constrained
Divine is the mind's eye
Soul's consciousness
More than man's
Than thine own O Lord!

Soul-Bond

When it so happens to some one
It really happens to him
Others' pain or their pleasure
Ought also be our treasure
For one to be detached
Philosophically be unlatched
One should feel still
To let it go or, go for kill
What happens to one
Has to two-way happen
Attached-detached

Paradox

Self over soul
Worldly goal
Soul over self
Bliss, no pelf
Rigmarole

Roll of seasons

Diwali Wish

Diwali wishes for one and all
Bright light in corners big and small
May the year bring more glee and cheer
For one and all near and dear
Let beaming faces and bright life
savour bliss with lessened strife
Diwali nights, Diwali days
Go on bliss-lit smooth pathways

Smile Away

Cool breeze enough chill
Ambience still has its fill
From life's lows and highs
My own thrills, my own sighs
Laugh out loud or cry shrill

Trick-O'-Treat

Halloween fever already in the air
Ghosts and witches to vanish in thin air
Eeriness articulated in arty accumulation
Pumpkins, spiders, brooms, webs,
tantrumEeeshhhhhhhhhhhhhhhhhhhhh!

Cooling Off

Morning glow
A virgin gesture
Of impending snow
On lumps and shoots
On water, on fire
On despair, desire
But telling truth
With no icing
Of wintry snow

Day & Night

Night's not only the dark side of it

Day may be night by some notches

Apparently yes, but as twilight

For either side it verily vouches

A Beautiful Day

This one's for you O, Vast Sky for giving cover

This one's for you O, Good Earth for food to nourish and sustain

This one's for you O, Leading Light for bounty of sun shine-shower

And O, benign Air for letting me wholesome flourish

A beautiful-beautiful day to remember for ever

Taking Turns

Four sentinels dying out

Prey to fall, about to fall

Autumn-spring it's all about

Leaves though but take the call

Leave moorings, gladly fall

Pithy Life

Lavender isn't just the leaves
Also, what the fall leaves
Grows green on being seen
Goes off colour, has a newer gleam
It's the life of well-lived leaves

Seep-Absorb

Dew from sky falls to settle
Shines, smiles, forms a ball
Lives-well, ends life's battle
Meeting earth with a fall

Hay-Day

Now listen O' ye persistent monsoon rains
It makes a difference to September and May
It's good if seasons overreach other's gain
Come you must but call it a day—Hey hey!

Springing Splashes

Wading through wavy waters
Jumping-thumping splashes
Spirits high on all quarters
All inhibition here crashes
Alike for noble and rotters

Drenched Gamuts

No it's not just a tune
Ah! musical crop's prune
Sing along, chime in well
Notes akin to notes jell
Sing ,hum or just croon
Hurray fulsome monsoon

Showered Out

Rain does the road enliven
Trampled, trodden, dubbed, driven
Also lets it cool its nerves
O' how saviour like it serves
Roughness gone, feel silken

Identification

Donno the breeze knows or no
Floating aroma confirms though
Something travels chugging along
Makes me feel here I belong
Let breeze never know, just flow

Boon

Sweet little rain-drop
Doesn't have any qualms
Is happy to make happy
Best of all the balms
On a sultry rainless day

Counsel

Creepy-creeper listens not
My counsel to it, set at naught
To grow leapy-flamy, and fraught
With swings of breeze and booze besot
Entwining tentacles woven as knot
But rather only on a trunk, taut
Promising the grip, not letting dropp't
Torn away, apart, or even draught
A swing's a swing, trunk's a trunk
Donno creeper got it right or not ?

Sultry

Mid-July, let fly, sky high, *arzoo*
Let cloud grunt loud, feel your *justjoo*
Brain fever heal pain singing *pihoo-pihoo*
Pluck yon heaven, sow it here, feel it here, *har-soo*!

Rain Check

Torrents and squalls of monsoons cool
Let'em stay home away from school
Children frolicking on terraces seen
Hot lava cake kurkure namkeen
Drenched at home, to hell with school!

Rains What?

Rains that one longs for are rains
Rains that one's soaked in are rains
Let float your paper boat
Scented air most sought
Rains that enliven one are rains

Rain Crave!

There's an onging fight
'tween clouds n light
'Sun you're too much!'
Hey clouds! Callout loud!
Drop rains, too much!

Summer Trick

You need your geyser in summers though
Take cold water from it than the tank above
To really enjoy your being under shower
To regain on yourself shining glow-glow

Pithy Warm

Summer heat setting in
Gulmohurs to burst soon
With *Amaltases* to soft paddle
Making fire for *Rhododendron*
Fire too blooms—soft petals
In a certain way—hang on, hang on!

Cooing

Cuckoo can never squeak shrill
Not at all on a morning in April
Blares' din highways abound in
She has treetops galore to coo and bill

Early Rains

April drizzle to pour for long
End to end on fringes strong
Feels and sounds nicer though
Summer should but warmer grow

Beginnings

Bougainvillea has all eyes, no nose
Bonsai no highs but only lows
Each one of us has none but us
To hold head high, no bows
Opposites aint meaningless, always
This is how the saying goes
Fear not the height if it dwarfs you
From lowliest ground a sprout grows

Spring Time

Wasps flitting in the air for sure
Herald the time for wheat to mature
Baisakhi round the corner, here
Boyz-n-galz 'Here-here! Here-here!'

Sad Scenario

Like foul smell to nose, stinked today the chill
Like screams n shrieks to ears, dinned today the chill
Like ugly fate to forehead, writ today the chill
Like thorns and spikes to lips, pricked today the chill
Giving new turn to chill, chilled today the chill
Like sultry heat of August, killed today the chill

Chill Set

Mirror or stone,
To their own!
Uninitiated callow showers
May not know
How to fall
Add to this a dash
Of haze-hash
A dab of mature mist
And it settles
For the day
Night is sure
To be compounded with
Still bigger threats
Heralding the onset of winter!

Rain Maker

No I didn't create the rain
It did drizzle, then a down pour
Even much before
I was thoroughly drenched
Like soggy chimera which
Comes and goes
Sometimes under cloud
Sometimes on sky nine
Sometimes soaked, seeped, surged or purged
Sometimes drenched, drained, drowned or deluged
Sometimes dry, drubbed, dead and done
Sometimes even bathing
In showers under the sun
On earth and sky's shining main
No I didn't create the rain

Hollow Thunder

Cloud, O'K—loud
Under cloud
Clamoring pain
And no rain
Thunder-thunder
All in vain
O, Lord Indra
Think again
Bury humid
In a shroud
Barren bane
Think again
Rain rain
Rain rain

Body & mind

Black & White

More or less of loaves and bites
More or less of floats and kites
More or less of wisps and light
More or less of less and more
More or less of things in sight

Posers To Mind

Light has a lighter quest
Less bright still seeks
Dark does have posers put
Shrill beam shatters, peeks
In between lies my dream
Sleep-walking mind speaks
Of wide-eyed escapades
Ogling, groping in gleam
To lull me into consciousness
To have my mind at rest
Answering dimly lit quest

Eyes Wide Open

Vehicles' blinkers blink to be seen
Eyes' blinkers make us see
Now I know meaning of seen
Now I know how blinking see
Blinking as blinkers

Stupid Mind

When good ideas drain
Out of the silly brain
To let brain keep doing
Some silly ideas remain

Situations

Cut-Outs

Were you there O, Silhouettes
Before the glistening, shiny rains fell?
Didn't even show thy snippets
Ere did blinding haze swell
You manifest out of nothing
Though I just lurked for you
Opened, you kept at me ogling!
You did form a rock—didn't you?
Of stony silence, shingling chime
You had a form, elevation too
But it's just a matter of time
When we get to see you—through

Curios

It's not the Grecian Urn
Yet does with spirits burn
Has a past and present too
Future will find it in a zoo
Of human indulgence and concern

Networking

Donno if poem gets likes
Or my pics carry spikes
To hook a friend
Just out of trend
Picspeak is dumb? Yikes!
Yo, yo, yupp. Shoo psyches!

Scene Sparkle

Dipping lights seem to travel deeper than their flight
Exploring beyond nature's award seems to be their right
Skies— dull, luminous, translucent, empty, or full bright
Watery sheen adding gleam to make a real delight

Sleepy Horizon

Of slopes and steep
A skyey peep
On to the earth
Beyond the slopes and steep
Into the blue-sky deep
There does a melted horizon sleep

Framed

How far after all
Can you see with naked eyes?
It's all laid bare, scattered to the skies
Only a scene does it make but
Unless to the picture I give a frame
Taming the vision is life to a shot
To hang for ever to charm
Even peeping out of the frame, Lo!
Whistling. Winking. Inviting. Hung-ho!

Waking Up!

A pesky nightmare
Hangs heavy on the mind
But should not scare
Dawn puts it in the grind
Reassurances then blare
For oneself to find
Making the vision clear
Then nightmares unwind
And no more scare
They fairy-look find

Pyrrhic Victory

I look at trophies, stoic, unassuming
Innocuous, ascetic, with no feeling
For them they sweat, kill and score
To win them, to flaunt more n' more

Two Kinds Of Smoke

Smoke rising good, than it billowing black
First, more pleasing; second, scary-stack
First, if seen in a jungle of wilderness
Raises hopes of some wellness
Second, if seen rising from a building
Sends the heart beating fast, ranting
Yes I refer, and have the wild-fires in mind
And you be aware of the blowing wind
Awaken, arise, change the course if need be
And make your home second smoke free
Douse fire, dampen, into the water soak
All shades of scary second variety smoke

Finding Myself

Blinkers here
Blinkers there
To regulate
Our watchfulness
Even ever-after-ever
Either caution
Of catastrophe
Or calamities
Calculating and phony
Chaotically blinking
Concerned only with
Lighted up cacophony
Even if it's a lighthouse
Of the grouted kind
Or a gadget put on snooze
Telling—I'm here to find

On Shore

None around to hold ground
A sea of passers by on shore
Cast no glance nor turn around
Dull cold shoulders me to abhor
Soft whispering to tell me more
Sweet nothings more and more

Mystic haze

Topsy-Turvy Mystic

It's always a tinkle that I touch
It's always a touch that I hear
It's always a ray that touches me
It's always a feel that I smell
It's only anger that I perspire
It's only blood that has my tears
It's only speaking that I taste
It's only shine that I eat
Don't think I've a skewed vision

Man & Mannequins

Tardy heights, silhouette's haze
Gentle slopes, shining phase
Earth's plains, depths and elevations
Nature to make many revealations
Seeking man searches, trods with craze

Roller Coaster

Isn't it fun to watch
rain drops fall
On electricity wires,
Hold and balance them there
Then getting heavier,
With other drops falling on them,
Beginning to slide the slope,
Stop awhile,
Roll again,
Fall finally
Even during falling,
If you have
A rollercoaster, or a swing
To rest on and ride, even for a shortwhile,
Adds a high
To a lowering down—intering
The watery grave

Idol-Worship

When I look at adorations
Pity their racy implorations
Honest reflections
Caustic reactions
Keep reaching them as returns
They stay calm like adorations

Bell-Tolls

People come and people go
Take their tides n' turns I know
Like musical-chairs' drop of tune
None too early none too soon
Whacked, announced—Here you go!

Happenstance

Beam too willing to strike
Shadow presto to abide
Nature allows no gap
Time, trance, no nap
All obtains, side by side

Beam Speak

The breezy song of flow
Gets to glittering glow
A ray slips over the rock
Recovering, begins to talk
With a hopeful face aglow

Word Builder

An update popped up
Soared into the skies
To be with stellar world
To look at me, an earthling
Teasing, tickling, tinkling, twinkling
'Come home, will give you more words'
I lure it in being with me
One time again
It tells me—"No thanks my Maker!
Am happy with as many words you made me with
And I make full sense. Do I not?
You have many words; I have just one maker!"

Pocketed Wisdom

Why should one think
And (thus) drive the 'why' out?
Isn't it better to
Die with 'why'
Well within?
Why make the 'why'
An empty inverted pocket?

Coy Outbursts

Poet's sensitive heart bears it all
You, me, him, hears it all
Love n' hate, bears it all
Good or bad, tears it all
Dark spots, smears it all
Faded zones, clears it all
Doom-despair, endears it all
Shrinks n' blues, tears it all
Pokes n' fun, jeers at it all
Far n' farther, nears at it all
Foul n' fiery fears it all
Joy n' gay cheers it all
Trust me, says 'Deswal'

Mirage

It was a dream
If I say come true
Will be *passé*
Not being a dream
One time more
If I say it was real
It will qualify
A fake or a farce
If I say it happened
It will negate its being
A dream!
Let a dream remain a dream!
Not to be explored n' seen
With eyes wide open

Nostalgia

A future day I cannot see
When reminiscent of times gone by
The day would dawn the same way
But the shine may not there be
Of the day that shone like the sun
A day that dawned, like it should be
If days make times memorable
Let'em nestle in the niches of memory

Ambitions

Finding the earth
Shrunk n' shriveled
No more fertile n' lush
I put on the Sky-bed
Some flower seeds
To grow and bloom
When goaded by
None other than
The formless clouds
The sky thundered
"Hey you, stop there!
Morro you gonna claim
All my galaxy n stars?
Head down to earth!
Bloke! Scoundrel!
Unworthy of earth!"
And I looked up
Agape! Again n again!

Tokens

Symbols have
A symbolism only
Of that which is
Unavailable
Obtaining
And
Unreal—mostly
Apologies for the two
onlys/onlies/onliz
Just a symbolism
No, not of apology
But only
See
I say
What I see only!

God Of Small Things

When a single flower blooms
In splendid glory solitude looms
Spreads happiness all around
Not being gazed, never found
Diminishing night
Gives up the slot
Having been done
But until I open
My window on it
Dawn happens not
Good to be charmed
With shine, snow, rain
Unexpected, just anew
Is more like a morning
A newer way dawning

Obeisance

Lost in daily humdrum banal din
Methinks we need practising faith
Otherwise, a single moment divine
In the cosmos scores eternal win
Of the self, the soul sayeth within
True, body needs practice and pulse
Seeks permanence through purgation
Not the saints' cup of tea—Meta-physics!
Nor mortals' bowl of poisonous sins
Sane Aristotle, pious Meera Bai
Sure comprised of flesh and bones!
No bones about God and His being
But only godliness, bliss experienced
And our abiding faith—to be practiced

Beautiful world

Gracious

A happy face's surely a happy face
Has enough poise, enough grace
Kindliness, compassion flow on it like barm
Sagaciousness, serenity keep their pace
Velvety, cushiony silky, shiny,—its yarn!

Velvety Thoughts

What ash is to smoke, word is to thought
One edifice, while myriad designs are fraught
Concrete, ductile, palpable, and soft
That which obtains is all that we've got
Velvet woven with thread and on loom
But what a finish my friend! It's brought

Daughters

Bud in the palm of the Gardener
He cleanses its soft petals
Like he does his daughter's cheeks
With his handkerchief
He holds the stem carefully to prune
Like he does his daughter's head
When he binds her tresses

Catharsis

Sloshed on the rose petal
Dew ball shining bright
Rolls down to the cusp
To hang for a moment, slight
On it more glow to settle
Ere it down to earth drops
Through hazed allies
Of conscious trance
Half in sleep
Fell, buried seep

Beaming Ray

Ray of hope
And of wish
Materializing
On petal's face
Brightens it
And brings it live
With a stretching
Of limbs and
Refreshing strings
Of bonding
Afresh

Gypsy time

Tick-Tock!

Time to heal
Time to steal
Time to herald
Time to feel
Time to let go
Time to show
Time to breathe
Time to go
Time does spread
Time is a thread
Time a bridge
Time to tread
Time is time
Yours and mine
Time it well
From time to time

Stay Put

From dawn to dusk
Through noon n' eve
No less a releigh of
Moments that leave
Traces of them
Their linkages
Even if temporal
Do not deceive

Moments Move

While being
Through the moment
Good or bad
One can come out
But has to be in it
Soon again
Through its wide
Casements
To look at it
Though detached
But attached still
For the moment
Leaves you not
While you may
Miss the moment
In its
Glory or grief
On which you have
No tabs
Watching the moment
Thus
May either enhance

Your pleasure
Or lessen
Your grief
Bestow best your grief
To the moment
To be happy
Commit your happiness
To the moment
To be happier!

Gimme A Moment

Time the way it should be
Lament is a moment
Laid back
Or laid down
Or let it slip from memory
For those
Who missed the bus
Yet regret missing it
Premium
To be paid
On payment
Not made

Sleep Talking

Speaking to myself
I am busy
Listening to myself
Still not one
Yet another
Seems done

Hunky-Dory

Floating music in the morning
A slice of life
Buttered
On both sides
To take you to the night
Signing lullabies
Lulled into melody
Music lives on, never dies
Notes to ears, to the soul
Sublime crescendo
Soft whispers
Sometimes even
Stillness speaks
And music keeps playing on

In Between

Lazy morns
Crispy nights
Lark shrieks
Elfish delights
Day divides
'Tween d' duo
Still makes
D' day bright

Intestate

The pain of fossils
One should feel
Gone dead long back
But suffering still
An identity for ever
In the same avatar
—listless!

Pearly Moments

Every drop is a drop in time
Forms, flows, falls, forgets
Beating both glory and grime
Moments grow into droplets
Running, relaying, rolling carpets

Time House

Tick-tock, tick tock, tick
Rhythm's life has to pick
Every moment every time
To keep engaging chime
Making its abode
Brick by brick

Another Name, Befitting?

I know not renaming the fog
All day's light it tends to hog
Suppresses it to minimum
Dazzle, glare to saddening dim
If I call it a wily spoil-sport
My intents to highlight abort
Not naming fog but blaming it
So I refrain from renaming it
Let names not mean to only mean
Let me bear with, not be mean
In naming nature all over again
What masters gave clear n' plain

Caressing

No it's not wheezing
But exhaling
With muffled wrapping
And dewy beads
On the curve of lips
Frozen with desire
To warm up to kissing
A breath of sunlight—dripping

Two-Zero-Thirteen

Two-thousand and thirteen
Another wish of shine n' sheen
Let me wish all well for you
For you being to myself true
All your blues may turn pink
All your sorrows finally sink
New earth, sky, sun n' moon
Dawn, dusk, morn, eve, noon
Entire world's world be yours
Nature's blessings, healings, cures
Gained aspirations hopes umpteen
Year ahead—two-zero-thirteen